WOOF! WOOF!

...TELLIGENCE AGENCY

CANINE INTELLIGENCE AGENCY

WOOF! WOOF! WOOF!

CIA'S MOST WANTED DOGS

MARK LEIGH

summersdale

CIA'S MOST WANTED DOGS

Summersdale Publishers Ltd
46 West Street
Chichester
West Sussex
PO19 1RP
UK

www.summersdale.com

Printed and bound in China

ISBN: 978-1-84953-295-2

Substantial discounts on bulk quantities of Summersdale books are available to corporations, professional associations and other organisations. For details telephone Summersdale Publishers on (+44-1243-771107), fax (+44-1243-786300) or email (nicky@summersdale.com).

3' 0"

2' 0"

WOOF! WOOF! WOOF!

CANINE INTELLIGENCE AGENCY

MOST
WANTED DOGS

From an original idea by
Mark Leigh & Mike Lepine

MARK LEIGH

ABOUT THE AUTHOR

The author and
Maxwell Woofington III

Surrey-based author Mark Leigh has written or co-written over forty humour and trivia books on subjects as diverse as millionaires, extraterrestrials, the Conservative Party and toilets (none of which are connected... although it sounds like they could be).

He has worked with the great and the good, including Julian Clary, Rolf Harris, Ade Edmondson, Des Lynam, Chris Tarrant and even Roy 'Chubby' Brown. TV projects have included scriptwriting for Joe Pasquale, Jeremy Beadle, Noel Edmonds, Hale & Pace, Brian Conley, Jimmy Tarbuck and Bobby Davro. His comedy novel *Dick Longg Saves the World!* is available on Kindle, while his works in progress include two film scripts.

Mark is an authority on badly behaved pets, being the owner of the naughtiest dog in the world, Maxwell Woofington III.

www.mark-leigh.com

INTRODUCTION

Canine Crooks, Pooch Perpetrators or Doggie Desperadoes…

Whatever you call them, this motley collection of mutts has one thing in common: they're all on the CIA's* Most Wanted list.

Sure, they may look affectionate, adorable and even amusing but appearances are deceptive. These dogs have been responsible for some of the most heinous and shocking crimes ever committed, from second-degree butt-sniffing and aggravated whining to receiving stolen dog biscuits. What's more, despite the best efforts of law enforcement officials and numerous 'Wanted' and 'Lost' posters pinned to trees, all these dogs are still at large. They could be hiding out anywhere: under your car, in your shed or even stretched out behind the couch…

So if you spot Spud, Scooby, L'il Fella or any of these other bow-wow bandits, you are advised not to approach them. Be warned; these dogs are clawed and dangerous!

*Canine Intelligence Agency

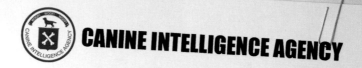

CANINE INTELLIGENCE AGENCY

Name:
Max

Aliases:
The Schmoo

Crime:
First-degree laziness

Notes:
Has a reputation for being bone idle and is believed to be lying low.
Is often seen in the vicinity of a quick brown fox.

CANINE INTELLIGENCE AGENCY

Name:
Buddy

Aliases:
Old Yeller

Crime:
Public nuisance offences

Notes:
Barks rowdily after the hours of darkness.
Also wanted for curfew violation (had been
ordered to stay indoors after 10 p.m.).

2' 0"

1' 6"

1' 0"

0' 6"

CANINE INTELLIGENCE AGENCY

Name:
Miffi

Aliases:
Dog Corleone

Crime:
Money laundering

Notes:
Responsible for most of the organised canine crime on the West Coast. Also known as the Dogfather.

CANINE INTELLIGENCE AGENCY

Name:
Scruffy

Aliases:
Lord Scrufton Of Bone Lane, Sir
Scruffington-Poochworthy

Crime:
Manufacture and supply of counterfeit
pedigrees

Notes:
Member of the Midtown Mongrels
crime syndicate.
Will also supply fake inoculation
papers to order.

CANINE INTELLIGENCE AGENCY

Name:
   Eddie

Aliases:
   Mr Ed

Crime:
   Begging with intent to cause guilt

Notes:
   Obtains treats by emotional blackmail.
   Also uses deceptive whining to con
   owners out of dog biscuits.

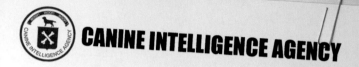

CANINE INTELLIGENCE AGENCY

Name:
Rex

Aliases:
King Clumsy

Crime:
Reckless endangerment

Notes:
Has a history of getting his head stuck in various railings, grilles, grates, fences and a can of Kibbles.
Serial attention-seeker.

CANINE INTELLIGENCE AGENCY

Name:
Baxter

Aliases:
Pipey McPiperson, Smokey, Sherlock

Crime:
Underage smoking

Notes:
Delusional: thinks he is a private investigator.
Also wanted for exposing puppies to second-hand smoke.

CANINE INTELLIGENCE AGENCY

Name:
Rebel

Aliases:
Chewbacca, The Footwear Fido

Crime:
Criminal damage and aggravated vandalism

Notes:
Wanted for the destruction of thirteen designer shoes and a pair of slingbacks. Thought to belong to the illegal gang The Manolo Mutts.

CANINE INTELLIGENCE AGENCY

Name:
Scooby

Aliases:
Scoobypoo

Crime:
Pooping in next door's garden with intent to endanger neighbourly relations

Notes:
Has complete disregard for property and boundaries.
Puts the 'poo' in 'pooch'.

CANINE INTELLIGENCE AGENCY

Name:
Hugo

Aliases:
The Hairy Cornflake

Crime:
Negligent hair shedding and malicious moulting

Notes:
Thought to have shed enough fur to create a whole new dog.
Also believed to go under the names of Fluffball and The Fluffinator.

CANINE INTELLIGENCE AGENCY

Name:
Casey

Aliases:
Itchy, Cootiekins

Crime:
Resisting flea powder

Notes:
Also wanted in connection with the illegal transportation of ticks and mites over state lines. Has previous conviction for tapeworm smuggling.

CANINE INTELLIGENCE AGENCY

Name:
Bailey

Aliases:
Nosey, The Nose

Crime:
Second-degree butt-sniffing

Notes:
Considered degenerate and dangerous. Has seventeen previous convictions under the Deviant Dogs Act.

CANINE INTELLIGENCE AGENCY

Name:
Ricky

Aliases:
Rock God, Ricky Sixx

Crime:
Imitating a member of Mötley Crüe with intent to defraud and deceive

Notes:
Also wanted for unlawfully impersonating the lead singers of Whitesnake and Europe.
Used to front the tribute band The Rolling Bones.

CANINE INTELLIGENCE AGENCY

Name:
Spud

Aliases:
Mucky Pup

Crime:
Unlawful distribution of mud inside a domicile

Notes:
Paw prints put him at the scene of a 2009 dirty duvet incident.
Also operates under the name of The Grubby Growler.

CANINE INTELLIGENCE AGENCY

Name:
Laddie

Aliases:
Doggie Woods

Crime:
Reckless driving

Notes:
Also wanted for hit and run.
Known by the very contrived alias of
Canine-Iron.
Still in possession of his balls.

CANINE INTELLIGENCE AGENCY

Name:
Bernie

Aliases:
Ol' Blue Eyes

Crime:
Aggravated howling

Notes:
The self-styled 'canine crooner'; acts in the mistaken belief that he can hold a tune.

Thinks he sings like Frank Sinatra. Actually sounds like Frank Bruno.

CANINE INTELLIGENCE AGENCY

Name:
Sasha

Aliases:
Mumsie

Crime:
Littering

Notes:
Gave birth to puppies in a public open space.
Was issued with a fixed penalty notice which she subsequently ate.

CANINE INTELLIGENCE AGENCY

Name:
Alexander

Aliases:
Xander, Big Al

Crime:
Resisting bath time

Notes:
Hates water. Hates shampoo even more. Can be identified by pungent doggie smell.

CANINE INTELLIGENCE AGENCY

Name:
Boris

Aliases:
Barfly, The Hooch Pooch

Crime:
Public intoxication

Notes:
Habitual underage drinker (in dog years).
Sobers up quickly following consumption of his hair.

CANINE INTELLIGENCE AGENCY

Name:
  Bertie

Aliases:
  Cry Baby

Crime:
  Being excessively needy

Notes:
  Continually follows owner around
  the house in a manner likely to cause
  annoyance.
  Known for perpetual hangdog
  expression.

CANINE INTELLIGENCE AGENCY

Name:
Champ

Aliases:
Twister

Crime:
Shaking himself dry in a violent manner likely to soak passers-by

Notes:
Should be considered dirty and extremely damp.
Eight outstanding warrants for his arrest issued by the Local Residents' Association.

CANINE INTELLIGENCE AGENCY

Name:
Bowser

Aliases:
ASBO Hound

Crime:
Antisocial behaviour

Notes:
Rings doorbells then runs away. Previous convictions for persistent barking after midnight and lamp-post loitering.

CANINE INTELLIGENCE AGENCY

Name:

Captain Pugwash

Aliases:

Stink Breath

Crime:

Using dog's breath in a manner likely to cause distress

Notes:

Recognised by his heavy panting. Also answers to the nickname Halitosis Hound.

CANINE INTELLIGENCE AGENCY

Name:
James

Aliases:
Jimmy The Dog

Crime:
Identity theft

Notes:
Master of disguise.
Impersonates owner for personal gain
and is able to go dog-food shopping on
his own.

CANINE INTELLIGENCE AGENCY

Name:
Sunshine

Aliases:
Cowardly Canine, Frightened Fido

Crime:
Being scared of nearly everything

Notes:
Fears include other dogs, cats, children, adults, cars, bicycles, squirrels, leaves and the rain.
Ironic nickname is Scaredy Cat.

CANINE INTELLIGENCE AGENCY

Name:
Harry

Aliases:
Houdini Hound

Crime:
Absconding from a secure establishment

Notes:
Escaped from three previous homes and tunnelled out of a boarding kennel.

Once made an escape rope out of a ripped-up dog blanket.

CANINE INTELLIGENCE AGENCY

Name:
Mack

Aliases:
The Demolisher, Mack The Ripper

Crime:
Criminal damage to bedding

Notes:
Has absolutely no sense of right or wrong.
Bad to the bone.

CANINE INTELLIGENCE AGENCY

Name:
Goldie

Aliases:
G-Man

Crime:
Removal of newspaper from letter box without the owner's prior permission

Notes:
Believed to be behind the abduction of twelve Sunday papers and colour supplements from March to September 2011.

CANINE INTELLIGENCE AGENCY

Name:
Freddy

Aliases:
Fred The Shred

Crimo:
Abusing a position of trust

Notes:
Was left alone for just five minutes.
Definitely not man's best friend.

CANINE INTELLIGENCE AGENCY

Name:
Lucy

Aliases:
Lucifer, Satan's Little Helper, Hell Hound

Crime:
Making strange guttural noises in a manner likely to sound demonic and scary

Notes:
Believed to be possessed. Do not approach (unless carrying a crucifix). Also sought by authorities for resisting an exorcism.

CANINE INTELLIGENCE AGENCY

Name:
Al Satian

Aliases:
Hacking Hound, The Pooch Programmer

Crime:
Cybercrime

Notes:
Responsible for writing malicious code and getting past the Pets at Home firewall to fraudulently obtain treats, dog toys, bedding, 200 boxes of dry dog food and a new collar and bell. Suffers from worms and also creates them.

CANINE INTELLIGENCE AGENCY

Name:
Peaches

Aliases:
Fifi, Bella, Debbie, Polly, Gill, Sara, Edie,
Sophie, Gaye, Adrienne, Millie and Rosie

Crime:
Bigamy

Notes:
May have been illegally married on at least
twelve separate occasions.
Stray; drifts from town to town looking for
sugar doggies.

CANINE INTELLIGENCE AGENCY

Name:
Milo

Aliases:
Johann Sebastian Bark

Crime:
Disturbing the peace

Notes:
Plays badly and loudly.
Currently in hiding but sought by
authorities to return and face the music.

CANINE INTELLIGENCE AGENCY

Name:
Captain Jack

Aliases:
Jolly Roger

Crime:
Video piracy

Notes:
Implicated in the distribution of counterfeit copies of *101 Dalmatians*, *Beethoven*, *Cujo*, *Benji*, *Digby*, *Turner and Hooch*, *Lassie Come Home*, *Lady and the Tramp* and *Best In Show*.

● REC

CANINE INTELLIGENCE AGENCY

Name:
Dixie

Aliases:
Dixibelle La La

Crime:
Grand theft blanket

Notes:
Also wanted for removing a duvet
without the owner's consent and
aggravated quilt theft.
Known accomplice of Crystal Smarty-
pants AKA The Sheet Thief.

CANINE INTELLIGENCE AGENCY

Name:
Cosmo

Aliases:
Vommo

Crime:
Failure to disclose information

Notes:
Owners were unaware that he suffered from chronic car sickness.
Also wanted on five counts of criminal damage (being violently sick on velour seats).

CANINE INTELLIGENCE AGENCY

Name:
Gonzo

Aliases:
The Ghost

Crime:
Speeding

Notes:
Clocked at 44 mph in a 20 mph zone.
Still on the run.

CANINE INTELLIGENCE AGENCY

Name:

L'il Fella

Aliases:

Barker Boy, B-Boy

Crime:

Receiving stolen dog biscuits

Notes:

Linked with Mafia-backed doggie snack distribution scam.
Also implicated in Bonio racketeering.

CANINE INTELLIGENCE AGENCY

Name:
Barney

Aliases:
Cat Lover

Crime:
Aiding and abetting

Notes:
Assisted Tabitha (AKA Claws) in the audacious 2010 Great Refrigerator Robbery. The Bonnie and Clyde of animal criminals.

CANINE INTELLIGENCE AGENCY

Name:
Lola

Aliases:
Lola McRingRing

Crime:
Making malicious phone calls

Notes:
Always on the dog and bone.
Also wanted for heavy panting and
then hanging up.

CANINE INTELLIGENCE AGENCY

Name:

Winona Cutie Pie

Aliases:

Champ

Crime:

Fraud by false representation

Notes:

Passes herself off as 'Best in Show'.
Claims to have also won first prizes
in these classes: Prettiest Bitch, Most
Attractive Puppy and Dog With The
Waggiest Tail.

CANINE INTELLIGENCE AGENCY

Name:
Charlie Boy

Aliases:
Tea Leaf

Crime:
Aggravated theft and grand larceny

Notes:
DNA evidence links him to audacious smash-and-grab raids at four high street jewellers.
Demonstrates a cavalier attitude towards other people's property.

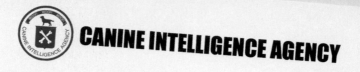

CANINE INTELLIGENCE AGENCY

Name:

Boomer

Aliases:

Jools

Crime:

Impersonating Julia Roberts

Notes:

Also wanted for fraudulently gaining access to a post-Oscars party and leaving paw prints in the wet cement on the Hollywood Walk of Fame.
Dominant bitch (and knows it).

THANK YOU

Mark would like to thank the following people for their suggestions, assistance and/or tea and chocolate Hobnobs:

Darin Jewel

Barney Leigh

Debbie Leigh

Polly Leigh

Mike Lepine

Anna Martin

PHOTO CREDITS

Bowser - Kevin Duffy
Captain Pugwash - Medvedev Andrey
James - Lobke Peers
Sunshine - Annette Shaff
Harry - Mark Herreid
Mack - Jeroen van den Broek
Goldie - Sonya Etchison
Freddy - Jeroen van den Broek
Lucy - Vladimir Kirienko
Al Satian - Nikolai Tsvetkov
Peaches - WilleeCole
Mllo - Palych
Captain Jack - Kelly Richardson
Dixie - Dorottya Mathe
Coomo - aerogondo2
Gonzo - Villiers Steyn
L'il Fella - Dee Hunter
Barney - Michael Pettigrew
Lola - Sue McDonald
Winona Cutie Pie - Viorel Sima
Charlie Boy - Maria Bell
Boomer - Carlos Restrepo
Thank You - IKO

If you're interested in finding out more about
our humour books follow us on Twitter:
@SummersdaleLOL

www.summersdale.com